The pictures that follow are all from the ancient royal palaces at Benin (now part of Nigeria). Except for the ivory face on this page, they were all cast in bronze. Portuguese adventurers appeared in Benin in 1485; soon they were trading bronze with the Beni and helping the king, who was called the Oba, in his wars. Bronze casting was said to have been introduced to Benin even earlier, by Igueghae from Ife, in the time of Oba Oguola, thought to be in the thirteenth century. Ife was about 100 miles north of Benin, and bronze casting may have been learned there from Arab traders. But none of these things are known for certain. Bronze plaques were made to adorn the Obas' palaces, and bronze statues were made for use in ceremonies. And, when an Oba died, bronze statues were made of his head for the new Oba's altar. You can see from these bronzes how the Obas dressed, the weapons of their warriors, pictures of their friends the Portuguese (of whom ten are on the crest worn here, and four are on the back cover). In time the Portuguese stopped coming to Benin. Then, in 1897, the British sent a party there to establish trade relations. The visitors were killed. The British then sent a punitive expedition, and the remarkable bronzes and ivories were discovered-or rediscovered-by Europeans and Americans.

The drummer on the front cover is in the Museum of Mankind, London; the chief on the back cover, making an offering to the Oba, is in the University Museum in Philadelphia. Drawings: N. Conkle & R. Zydycrn

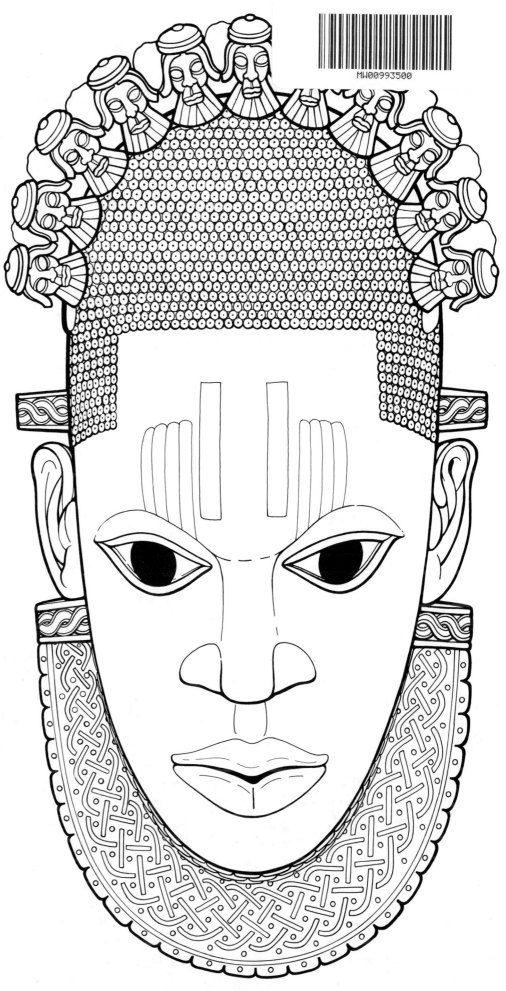

Museum of Mankind, London

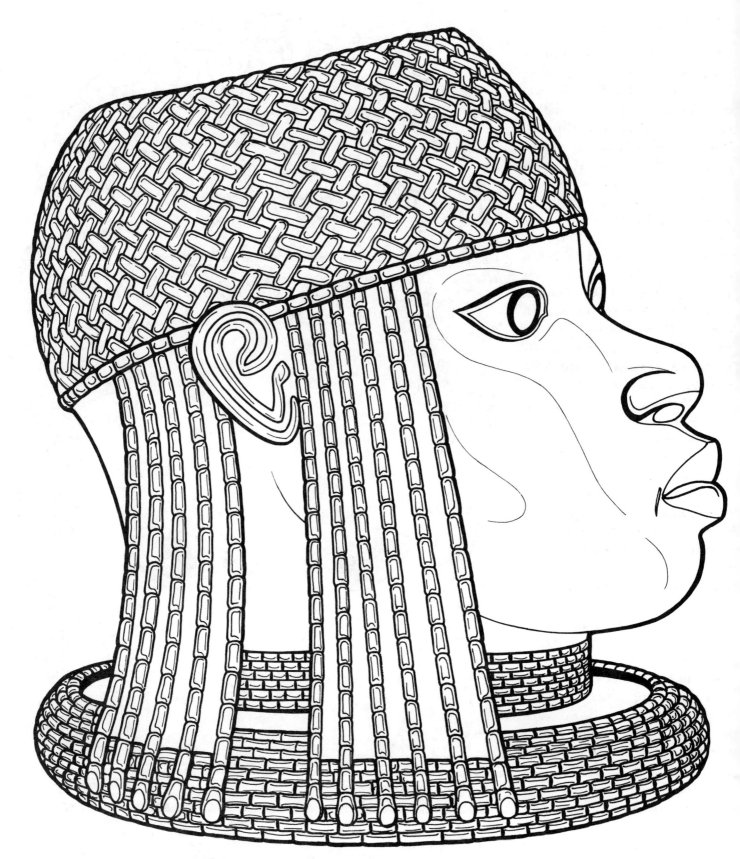

The Oba or King of Benin

About 1500 A.D.

Several Obas were probably the most powerful men in the world, for visiting Europeans wrote that they were able to raise armies of 100,000 warriors in 24 hours, something no European or Asiatic king could dream of in those days.

Museum of Primitive Art, New York

The Oba goes for a ride

The Iyoba or Queen Mother

National Museum, Lagos

About 1550 A.D.

The Queen of Benin

Females almost never appear on Benin plaques. This is rare and late.

Two leopards,
symbols of the
Oba's power

Städtisches Museum für Völkerkunde, Frankfurt

The Oba's Palace

There was a bronze bird on top, and a bronze python running down the turret front. The roof was shingled, and bronze plaques showing

Benin City

Portuguese visitors were attached to the posts. The guards' spears have broken off. Fan bearers provided "air-conditioning"—it was hot!

Museum für Völkerkunde, Berlin

Museum of Man, London
About 1600 A.D.

Visitors from the North

Feathered hats like these are still worn by the
Fulani, the Emir's bodyguards in Northern Nigeria.

Museum of Mankind, London   About 1600 A.D.

The Oba's Horn Blower

He would blow his horn when someone was beheaded; this was done at the *Ugie-ivie* ceremony honoring the Oba's beads. This was made at about the same time that King Henry VIII was having similar rites performed in England.

Museum of Mankind, London

Ofoe,
the Messenger of Death

National Museum, Benin City

About 1500 A.D.

Opposite
The Oba
Full Reg
About 160

A Chief of Benin and a Warrior

They both wear necklaces of leopards' teeth and headdresses of shell.

National Museum, Lagos

A dance representing a battle against the sky

About 1500 A.D.

The Oba in a High Coral Collar & a Beaded Cap

The St. Louis Art Museum

About 1650 A.D.

The Drummers

About 1650 A.D.